THE TREASURE HUNT

Joshua Jones

Scripture quotations are taken from the Holy Bible, New Living Translation, copyright ©1996, 2004, 2015 by Tyndale House Foundation. Used by permission of Tyndale HousePublishers, Carol Stream, Illinois 60188. All rights reserved.

Dedication

For my Lord and Savior Jesus Christ and my beautiful twin daughters Lilly Anne and Layla Jane. Two of the many treasures that have been given by God.

Acknowledgments

I would like to start off by thanking God for the talent that He placed in me to write. I would like to express my gratitude to my friend and mentor David Mattocks who has helped me with the publishing of this book. A big thanks to pastor David Hintz and pastor Bruce Clark who have been brothers in the faith and such sources of encouragement along this journey. To my mother Debra Jones and my father Jeffrey Jones who have sacrificed so much for me and for that I am forever grateful. To my brother Lonnie King who took me on my first mission trip which was a treasure hunt for the kingdom. Finally, I would like to thank all the ones who have encouraged me in my walk with the Lord. May the Lord bless you and keep you.

Preface

Throughout my journey in life, I have been stirred to write daily devotionals to the Lord. I would find later in life that others were really encouraged by them. Each one that I have written has been inspired by the Holy Spirit who has motivated me to keep going. It's an honor for me to be writing on behalf of the Lord and to help others in their walk with Jesus Christ.

Psalms 40:2 *"He lifted me out of the pit of despair, out of the mud and the mire. He set my feet on solid ground and steadied me as I walked along."*

Day 1

The Treasure Hunt

I remember the first mission trip I ever went on. As we left for Georgia from Michigan, I saw that there was a path that the Lord had prepared for us. It was my first real experience in stepping out in faith, and when I did it I saw that God had everything taken care of. There is excitement in following God! He awakens us by the power of His Holy Spirit to give birth to new life and new awakenings each day. I would learn that there was an amazing story that God had written about me, and if I would dig deeper, I would find the treasure of knowing Christ. The love that we are given first comes from God. As He fills us more each day, we are awakened to share the Good News that Jesus is alive and that He loves us. The name Jesus Christ is a treasure and all who find Him are truly blessed.

Colossians 2:3 *"In him lie hidden all the treasures of wisdom and knowledge."*

Personal Reflections

How can you hit the streets in the marketplace or at your work to share the Good News of Jesus?

What creative ways can you spread God's love to others this week?

_____

_____

_____

_____

_____

_____

_____

_____

_____

_____

_____

_____

_____

_____

_____

_____

Day 2
His Hands and Feet

I remember one time a friend of mine brought a prayer request for a job to my attention. As we began to pray, I felt the Lord nudging my heart saying, "Who do you know that is hiring?" As I got back home, I thought to myself, "Wow Lord you answer your prayers through your people!" God has equipped us to do every good work, and as we see a need in our community, or in our family, we can be the saints that go marching in to their rescue. God today is asking us to be His hands and feet and be the boots on the ground. We each can play our part in the role of serving and helping others in need. As you ask God for wisdom, keep your eyes and ears open. He may just be speaking an answer to that prayer through you.

Hebrews 13:21. *"may he equip you with all you need for doing his will. May he produce in you, through the power of Jesus Christ, every good thing that is pleasing to him. All glory to him forever and ever! Amen"*

Personal Reflections

How can you better help serve those who are in need?

Reflect and write of a time God used you as an answer to someone's prayers.

_____

_____

_____

_____

_____

_____

_____

_____

_____

_____

_____

_____

_____

_____

_____

_____

Day 3

The Father's Love

The day we were born was a moment when everything changed in our lives, and the lives of those around us. We were each placed into our mother's arms from the womb and let out our first cry. It was also the moment that God heard our cry here on Earth. I can only imagine what it felt like for the Father to see us in our human form. In God's word it says that He knew us before we were formed. Throughout life there would be trials and how it must have hurt the Father's heart to see us fall. Then one day everything would change. The day that we accepted Christ into our hearts and began in our walk with God would be the beginning of a journey and awakening in our soul. As we grow in our walk with Jesus, we find that we long for His presence. His goodness and love protect and help lead us back to the path of innocence when we were first formed.

Galatians 1:15 *"But even before I was born, God chose me and called me by his marvelous grace. Then it pleased him."*

Personal Reflections

In what ways do you see the uniqueness of being fearfully and wonderfully made?

Spend some time writing a letter to the Father to tell Him of your love for Him.

_____

_____

_____

_____

_____

_____

_____

_____

_____

_____

_____

_____

_____

_____

_____

Day 4

Freedom From Within

When we go from having a sin conscious to having a God conscious, we go from looking for direction to knowing we are being directed. It is God's Spirit that leads, and as we learn to do what is pleasing to the Holy Spirit, our walk with God improves dramatically. Yes, it does take sacrifice, but the reward of knowing Christ is well worth it. The Lord lifts His countenance up on us His children. As we sit at the feet of Jesus, we learn to follow down the path that leads to eternal life. Heaven awaits us one day and there will be a reward greater than any of us can imagine. Until that day comes, we can rejoice in the Spirit of the Lord, for where His Spirit is there is freedom. His grace covers us and will lift us up even in the deepest valleys.

Galatians 5:16 *"So I say, let the Holy Spirit guide your lives. Then you won't be doing what your sinful nature craves."*

Personal Reflections

In what ways have you sensed a change in the movies you watch or the music you listen to?

Where in your life can you see how God has cleansed you from the inside out?

_____

_____

_____

_____

_____

_____

_____

_____

_____

_____

_____

_____

_____

_____

_____

_____

Day 5

Amazing Grace!

Through the toils and snares of life, we see amazing grace. It's not just a song, but it's a story of a beautiful Saviour who is here and willing to sit beside us to lead us beside the still waters. This road that we are on, while although may be at times tough, has an eternal hope. The treasure of a home in Heaven to be with the one who was with you and saved you is worth whatever we face here. God's beauty is here now. We have the opportunity and the freedom to step out on the water and meet with Jesus. Just to sit at His feet and worship the living God we find a pure joy that will last through the ages. Throughout our life there was, is, and will be a Saviour named Jesus that will walk beside us. If we open our hearts to Him, we will feel His hand over our lives leading us down paths of righteousness for His name's sake.

Ephesians 2:8 *"God saved you by his grace when you believed. And you can't take credit for this; it is a gift from God."*

Personal Reflections

Listen to the song Amazing Grace today. How does it speak to you?

_____

_____

_____

_____

_____

_____

_____

_____

_____

_____

_____

_____

_____

_____

_____

_____

Day 6

Speaking Life

We each have a voice given to us by God and our voice matters. God is calling out to us to speak to Him in the secret place and to come into a relationship with Jesus Christ. We have the power to speak life over ourselves, over our families, and over others. As we speak of the goodness and love of God our atmosphere begins to change. We see that what truly matters is to know Christ, and when we come and draw into His secret place we come in communion with His Holy Spirit. You have a story and a testimony that is powerful. There is someone right now that if you will share your story with, and tell them about Jesus, they will be set free. He has given us a miracle of a voice, but it is up to us to choose the words that we speak. Today choose to speak blessings over life by the power of prayer and worship before the Father.

Ephesians 4:15 *"Instead, we will speak the truth in love, growing in every way more and more like Christ, who is the head of his body, the church."*

Personal Reflections

Write a prayer today speaking life over yourself and others.

What platforms has God given you to share your testimony?

_____

_____

_____

_____

_____

_____

_____

_____

_____

_____

_____

_____

_____

_____

_____

_____

Day 7

Love Poured Out

The same Spirit that raised Christ from the dead lives in you. His reckless love has pushed passed barriers, and brought us who were once lost, home. We now have been adopted into a family by the love of Christ. His grace that was poured out over the cross has come to be the cornerstone to our faith. Jesus the same yesterday, today, and forever has the power to save and liberate those who were once captive. There are rivers of living water that we can take part in now. Jesus said that those who believe in Him would never hunger or thirst. We each can press in towards the presence of God. It is in the power of the Holy Spirit that we are awakened to see God's glory in our life. From our children's smile to God's creation the Holy Spirit opens our eyes to see God's grace which is all around us.

John 20:31 *"But these are written so that you may continue to believe that Jesus is the Messiah, the Son of God, and that by believing in him you will have life by the power of his name."*

Personal Reflections

In what ways can you draw close to God today?

How has God brought you back home into His presence?

_____

_____

_____

_____

_____

_____

_____

_____

_____

_____

_____

_____

_____

_____

_____

_____

Day 8

The Knitting Station

There have been over 117 billion people who have lived on planet Earth according to the latest statistics. Out of these people created there have never been any two people who have been created the same. It's truly amazing when you think about how God designed each of us with a unique set of fingerprints, and a special set of features, that were unlike any other human ever created. It testifies to the goodness and awe of God and how we each are fearfully and wonderfully made. There is a unique set of gifts and talents that God placed in you that when you find them it's as if you've found a treasure. The testimony that we've been given is a story that was given to us from the Lord. That same testimony that lives inside of you is a story of redemption and is a testimony of victory. The day when we met our Lord and Saviour and everything as we knew it changed. Today, if you give your heart to the author and finisher of your story, you will begin to see that same story that was written before the foundation of the world.

Psalms 139:14 *"I will praise thee; for I am fearfully and wonderfully made: marvellous are thy works; and that my soul knoweth right well."*

Personal Reflections

In what ways can you see the miracles in God's creation?

What unique talents or gifts do you believe God has given you?

_____

_____

_____

_____

_____

_____

_____

_____

_____

_____

_____

_____

_____

_____

_____

_____

Day 9

He Was Always There

Someone gave a word one time that really resonated with me. He said, "Every time I reached back for God, I found He was always there." Joshua the prophet was given a big assignment after Moses had passed. He was to not only to lead the Israelites but give them hope and encourage them that God was with them. Joshua had received a word that the Lord had given Moses, and later from the Lord Himself about the task ahead. Joshua needed this confirmation to strengthen his faith for the battles that awaited him. Throughout life there is one who never changes or casts a shifting shadow. He is faithful even during times when we are not and will never leave us or forsake us. Today you are not alone, you have a God who loves you and knows the plans He has for you. They are plans for good and not for disaster, to give you a future and a hope. Open your heart to the Lord today. Draw close to God and He will draw close to you.

Jeremiah 29:11 *"For I know the plans I have for you," says the lord. "They are plans for good and not for disaster, to give you a future and a hope."*

Personal Reflections

Reflect and write briefly of the time when you were once lost. Do you see how God rescued you?

Do you see where God was always there now looking back?

_____

_____

_____

_____

_____

_____

_____

_____

_____

_____

_____

_____

_____

_____

_____

_____

_____

Day 10

God Winks

Each week at our Bible study we get the honor and privilege to share in the testimonies of God's hand over our lives. Some call them God winks, or God's fingerprints, but they are living testimonies of the miracles that are found in the right hand of the Father. When we hear these testimonies, they strengthen our faith opening our eyes to the fact that Jesus is not only real but is alive and with us. Whenever I get to share my own personal testimony of the goodness of God I bubble over with excitement much like a kid because I know God intervened that day in my life. He loves every one of us so much and shows these miracles across the footprints of each of our lives. As footprints in the sand, we can see the imprints of the Lord's hand across our lives. How a God so big, who created the Heavens and the Earth, can still care enough about us testifies to the awe and wonder of who He is.

Psalms 8:3-4 *"When I look at the night sky and see the work of your fingers the moon and the stars you set in place what are mere mortals that you should think about them, human beings that you should care for them?"*

Personal Reflections

What "God Winks" have you witnessed this month?

Reflect and write a divine appointment where God had you encounter His grace.

_____

_____

_____

_____

_____

_____

_____

_____

_____

_____

_____

_____

_____

_____

_____

_____

_____

_____

Day 11

Empty Slate

It is only through the forgiveness of God that I can look inside of myself and know I am forgiven. The slate wiped clean the day Jesus went to that cross. With a burst of light, Heaven came to resurrect our king. Today He calls each one of us to lay our burdens down and know that it is in His name where our help comes from. God's mercies renew each morning and with this day that we have been given, let us extend grace to ourselves and to others. No matter where you are God will meet you and will help you if you soften your heart. The price has already been paid for you to be set free. Today walk free knowing that God loves you and is for you.

Isaiah 1:18 *"Come now, let's settle this," says the lord. "Though your sins are like scarlet, I will make them as white as snow. Though they are red like crimson, I will make them as white as wool."*

Personal Reflections

How have you experienced forgiveness from God?

How have you come to new life since coming to Christ?

_____

_____

_____

_____

_____

_____

_____

_____

_____

_____

_____

_____

_____

_____

_____

_____

_____

_____

_____

Day 12

Asking For Wisdom

The more we acknowledge Him in all our ways the more we will find our steps are being directed. All of us search for more of an understanding about life but many times we do not seek with our whole heart the one who holds all the answers. Even though we each fall short, we have a God who gives grace and peace, but we must ask Him. Learning to listen more to that still small voice, and not our own, comes from seeking first the kingdom of God and His righteousness. Today there is freedom in the name of Jesus. Today if there are any burdens you are carrying lay them all down at the feet of the one who came to carry them. You will find that the more you come to Him, even in your shortcomings, the more you will find that He will cleanse you and help you start again.

James 1:5 *"If you need wisdom, ask our generous God, and he will give it to you. He will not rebuke you for asking."*

Personal Reflections

In what ways can you practice more listening for the voice of God?

In what areas of your life can you seek wisdom from God? Write and ask Him.

_____

_____

_____

_____

_____

_____

_____

_____

_____

_____

_____

_____

_____

Day 13

Blessed Assurance

Our faith develops when we begin to believe, stand on, and thank God for what He has already done. We can rest in the blessed assurance that Jesus is with us and is for us. The promises of a hope and a future are in His hands and as we look to Him our faces will not be ashamed but will be radiant with joy. It takes humility to ask for help, but with humility comes wisdom. Sometimes we think we need to have everything in place first before we come to God, but we forget that it is in our brokenness and humility we find grace. He puts together our broken pieces and makes a masterpiece giving beauty for ashes. God wants us to humble ourselves and meet with Him today in the secret place. You have a direct line to God by the power of the Holy Spirit. What a blessed assurance it is to know that we can trust God with our lives, and He will show us the way.

John 14:6 *"Jesus told him, "I am the way, the truth, and the life. No one can come to the Father except through me."*

Personal Reflections

In what areas today can you practice humility?

Do you recall a time you humbled yourself and got the answer you were looking for? Write about it.

_____

_____

_____

_____

_____

_____

_____

_____

_____

_____

_____

_____

_____

_____

_____

_____

_____

_____

Day 14

Floodgates Of Healing

Feeling the Holy Spirit come into your heart for the first time is a feeling unlike any other. For myself, the door to my heart and my mind had been closed for so long, that when the light hit it birthed an awakening unlike any other. A flood of a warm healing from the presence of God's Spirit came and when it did it gave new life to my dry bones. The woman who reached for the hem of Jesus garment knew this. She knew that just a simple touch from the Lord, and everything would change in her life. One problem I've noticed today is that we are not hungry enough for God. God promises that when we seek after Him with our whole heart we will find Him. What that means is that we must die to self and seek the liberty that comes from the Holy Spirit. What is it that the Lord is telling you to lay down that is holding you back from running the race? Today press forward towards Jesus who is our treasure and our reward.

Matthew 9:22 *"Jesus turned around, and when he saw her he said, "Daughter, be encouraged! Your faith has made you well." And the woman was healed at that moment."*

Personal Reflections

Write or share a testimony today of where God has or is healing you now.

What is the Lord putting on your heart to lay down today?

_____

_____

_____

_____

_____

_____

_____

_____

_____

_____

_____

_____

_____

_____

_____

_____

Day 15

A New Day

With each new day comes a new beginning. The skies today are displaying the Lord's craftsmanship and with this freedom is here. It's ok to start again and know that you can walk in the forgiveness of God. As we move forward throughout life, we will begin to see that each new day is a living miracle given to us by a living God. The freedom given to us by the blood of Jesus should be celebrated each day. The day that everything changed when a beautiful Saviour named Jesus stepped into our darkness and brought us into His marvelous light should be cherished in our hearts. Our days, like our hairs, are all numbered, and we each can rejoice in this day the Lord has made. God's love is amazing and if we begin to walk in that love, we will see that it is ok to start again. Today ask the Lord to create in you clean hands and a pure heart. Step into the forgiveness of God and with this gift that you have been given show that forgiveness and love towards yourself and others. Rejoice!

Lamentations 3:23 *"Great is his faithfulness; his mercies begin afresh each morning."*

Personal Reflections

Spend time outside today in awe of the creation that God has given us.

Ask the Lord today to create in you clean hands and a pure heart. Write and reflect on a prayer to Him.

_____

_____

_____

_____

_____

_____

_____

_____

_____

_____

_____

_____

_____

_____

_____

_____

_____

Day 16

Overflowing Love

God's love that overflows in our hearts allows us to focus on Jesus and the beauty of this world that is all around us. What a day it was when we felt the presence of the Lord come into our lives and carry us to new life on His shoulders home. Like the good Shepard we now have the freedom to share this newfound joy with others. We can be the vessels God uses to fulfill the purpose of the Lord, which is to seek and save that which was lost. There is no condemnation for those who are in Christ Jesus. God is waking us this day to a mercy that renews with a love that calls us into freedom. It's the same Spirit, that raised Christ from the dead, that gives us the power to overcome our sin. We each still have struggles, but God remains faithful and kind with us through them all. This is why His love will never be matched by anything we will ever see or hear.

John 11:25 *"Jesus told her, "I am the resurrection and the life. Anyone who believes in me will live, even after dying."*

Personal Reflections

What scriptures has God highlighted for you today?

Spend time writing out some of your favorite scriptures that God has highlighted for you.

_____

_____

_____

_____

_____

_____

_____

_____

_____

_____

_____

_____

_____

_____

_____

_____

_____

Day 17

The Gift

To hear someone say that you've made a difference in their life is a feeling unlike any other. Just to know that you can be used for God's purpose here on Earth is humbling to say the least. Each of us have something to contribute today. With the gift of salvation and a new life in Christ we each have a message that needs to be delivered. Today the harvest is plenty and filled with those who need Jesus. You can be that light that makes a difference to change not only someone's life but the lives of those around them. Whether it be a call to let someone know they are not alone, or a hand stretched out to help someone in need, you can be that messenger of hope. There is new life today in the name of Jesus and out of our mouth we can speak that life over ourselves and others.

Matthew 9:37 *"He said to his disciples, "The harvest is great, but the workers are few."*

Personal Reflections

Write about the hope of God that lives in you that encourages you each day.

Who can you extend a hand or message to let them know they are not alone?

_____

_____

_____

_____

_____

_____

_____

_____

_____

_____

_____

_____

_____

_____

_____

Day 18

Childlike Faith

One of the fondest memories of my childhood was the feeling of anticipation to go play and have fun with my friends. We would ride our bikes to the playground for the day to play sports and just be kids. Today I believe that the Lord is restoring that childlike innocence by the power of His Spirit. God turns our mourning into dancing and lifts our heaviness to replace it with His peace. Each day we can rejoice in a day that God has made just for us. He has given us authority by the name of Jesus over everything that hinders us and today there is freedom. We can begin to run in the garden and share with others in the hope that is found in Jesus Christ. The commands that God gives are a safeguard and He is a Father that protects His children.

Matthew 18:4 *"So anyone who becomes as humble as this little child is the greatest in the Kingdom of Heaven."*

Personal Reflections

What ways can you become as a child again?

Spend time reflecting and writing about a time when things were simple.

_____

_____

_____

_____

_____

_____

_____

_____

_____

_____

_____

_____

_____

_____

_____

_____

_____

Day 19

The Calm In The Storm

There is one who walks beside us and who leads us beside the still waters. While there may be different storms throughout our lives, there is one who is with us and promises to never leave. Jesus, the good Shepard, is one who remains the same yesterday, today, and forever. He stands at the door of our hearts knocking. Today, if we will let Him in, He will come and make a home with us. Trusting in God with all our heart is a process but as we move forward we will see that it is in Him where our help comes from. Every good gift comes from the Father of lights. As we acknowledge Him more in all our ways, we will see that His goodness is all around us. The goodness of God is a gift and a fruit of the Holy Spirit which is available for all of us to experience.

Psalms 34:8 *"Taste and see that the lord is good. Oh, the joys of those who take refuge in him!"*

Personal Reflections

Is there a storm in your life that you are in today?

Ask and write to God seeking wisdom and peace even in the storm.

_____

_____

_____

_____

_____

_____

_____

_____

_____

_____

_____

_____

_____

_____

_____

Day 20

Power In The Blood

From just a touch of the Lord's presence everything can change. The transforming and healing power of the presence of God can break down strongholds and set a captive free. While we move through life there are things that may weigh us down, but God is faithful. If we will come into His presence through the Bible, prayer, or worship, we will begin to feel the comfort from the one who came to comfort us. God is a helper and a shield to all who put their hope and trust in Him. Just to know that Jesus loves you and has forgiven you gives you a strength to persevere through this life. There is no one who is too far beyond the reach of God. God is love and that love is patient and kind. This perfect love is here for us today. We each have the ability and opportunity to press into the love of God.

Matthew 14:36 *"They begged him to let the sick touch at least the fringe of his robe, and all who touched him were healed."*

Personal Reflections

What areas of your life can you plead the blood of Jesus over today?

Write out a prayer asking the Father to cover you with the blood of Jesus.

_____

_____

_____

_____

_____

_____

_____

_____

_____

_____

_____

_____

_____

_____

_____

Day 21

Power To Save

Just as the light of God lit up the grave and resurrected His son Jesus, so God has the power to save a life that is lost. This life-giving power can bring to life even the most lost. No matter how far you think you've wandered off the path, God still loves you. He first loved us with a Father's love and has plans for a future and a hope. He simply asks us to turn to Him and humble ourselves. If we do this and turn from our sin, He will heal us and show us life and life more abundantly. God came with His arms stretched wide and His heart open so that not one of us should perish. All of us have sinned and fallen short of the glory of God. Today we have been forgiven by God's love that was poured out over the cross and the price of our sin has been paid. We can rejoice and know that we are sons and daughters of God, by standing on the foundation of Jesus Christ.

1 John 4:10 *"This is real love not that we loved God, but that he loved us and sent his Son as a sacrifice to take away our sins."*

Personal Reflections

Reflect and write a brief testimony of a time when you felt the love of God.

What are some of the things that come to mind that God has saved you from?

_____

_____

_____

_____

_____

_____

_____

_____

_____

_____

_____

_____

_____

_____

_____

Day 22

Never Alone

There is a lot of power in knowing that God is with you and that He loves you beyond all you can think or imagine. God can open our eyes to see the ones that are there to help us. Today know that you belong to a family. There is an army of believers who share in the same salvation of the living God. God is faithful and will never leave us or forsake us. As we look to the author and finisher of our faith, He will give us the strength and courage to find new friends who will become family in the faith. We are never alone God is with us and will continue the work that He started before we were born.

Matthew 18:19 *"For where two or three gather together as my followers, I am there among them."*

Personal Reflections

Who is it that God is putting on your heart that is a source of wisdom?

Is there someone in your church or community that God is putting on your heart to reach out to? How?

_____

_____

_____

_____

_____

_____

_____

_____

_____

_____

_____

_____

_____

_____

_____

_____

Day 23

Becoming As A Child

A woman at our church shared a testimony of being healed from her diabetes. In her testimony she revealed how the pastor's granddaughter, who is five years old, had been praying for her to be healed. It's amazing how the Lord protects and blesses those with childlike faith. This little girl saw a need for healing and knew that God alone could heal her, so she prayed. Not only did she pray but she didn't stop praying, she continued to pray for her to be healed and God set her free by healing her of the diabetes. It's amazing how, when we come to God in faith, He rewards us as we diligently seek Him. Our God has the power to heal and restore that which is broken. When we walk by faith and pray to God knowing that He is with us, there is no end to the possibilities. New life begins with those whose faith and hope is in the Lord. When we humble ourselves and come to Him in prayer, we will see life begin to change all around us. Your prayers for others no matter what your age or how long you've been walking with the Lord are important because you are praying in faith that God hears them.

Psalms 116:6 *"The lord protects those of childlike faith; I was facing death, and he saved me."*

Personal Reflections

What ways in your life could you draw closer to God and seek His will?

Write out a prayer today for someone who you know needs healing.

_____

_____

_____

_____

_____

_____

_____

_____

_____

_____

_____

_____

_____

_____

_____

_____

Day 24

Soaring Above

While most birds will seek shelter from the storm, the eagle is the only one who flies above the clouds. Once above the storm, the eagle is clear of the rough winds and its flight becomes smoother. We each have storms throughout the course of our life. As we begin to stand with courage to face the raging winds of our battle there is one who is faithful and fights with us. The battle belongs to the Lord. As our faith increases over our testimony, we see that during the storm is when God is the closest. Like the footprints in the sand our God carries us and helps us mount on wings like eagle's. Will it be difficult at times in life? Yes. Will there be times when we feel alone? Yes. God is faithful. He is faithful to the ones He loves and will be beside us every step of the way. Jesus is the ever-present help in times of trouble and is the one who is faithful to give us the ability to fly through, and soar above the storm.

Isaiah 40:31 *"But those who trust in the lord will find new strength. They will soar high on wings like eagles. They will run and not grow weary. They will walk and not faint."*

Personal Reflections

In what areas of your life do you need to trust in the Lord more?

Reflect and write on a time where God helped you persevere through a storm that you faced.

_____

_____

_____

_____

_____

_____

_____

_____

_____

_____

_____

_____

_____

_____

_____

_____

Day 25

Our Passion

One of the most beautiful things about God's love is coming into a relationship with Him. Each person has their own unique relationship with God and it's a beautiful thing. King David wrote it best by saying "Your unfailing love is better than life itself." The love of God is here for each one of us. When we come into an intimate relationship with God, we begin to see it is He who our hearts long for. It is the one who was with us and that never left. God's peace that passes all understanding comes in knowing you have a relationship with Jesus Christ. It's knowing that God loves you so much and has created you in a way that only He could do. This love is so great that even in our brokenness and sin He still loves, calling us back into the relationship where we cry out Abba Father!

Psalms 67:1 *"May God be merciful and bless us. May his face smile with favor on us."*

Personal Reflections

Spend time today in the secret place with God.
How did you feel after?

Do you have more peace when trusting God? In what
ways?

_____

_____

_____

_____

_____

_____

_____

_____

_____

_____

_____

_____

_____

_____

_____

_____

Day 26

Fingerprints Of God

As we lift our head to the beauty and awe of another day, we see God's grace. It's painted across the sky and the waters. The birds rise early to sing of another day that the Lord has made. What joy awaits us! The Lord has painted across our lives as well. His beauty of a day with eyes to see His hand and ears to hear His voice is a gift. As we go about our day, we see that there are many gifts and fruits for us to enjoy. We can taste and see that the Lord is good! This radiant joy that is given by God breathes new life and new hope to all of us His children. Whatever it is that we face today we have a helper. The Holy Spirit illuminates our minds and our hearts to focus on the blessings of God. As we pour our hearts out to Jesus in thanksgiving for all He has done we will see that we have only just begun to experience all the awe and wonder that is God.

Psalms 34:8 *"Taste and see that the lord is good. Oh, the joys of those who take refuge in him!"*

Personal Reflections

How can you spend time this week meditating on the miracles of God in His creation?

Write out some of the miracles that God lets us experience each day.

_____

_____

_____

_____

_____

_____

_____

_____

_____

_____

_____

_____

_____

_____

_____

_____

Day 27

Greatest Love

The love of Christ can never be fully understood but we know that He loves each of us with a Father's love. He is a Father to the fatherless, and a refuge to all who put their faith and hope in Him. God is love. A love that is so perfect that it would stop at nothing even if it meant laying His life down so we could walk free. Understanding the level of forgiveness by the love God showed gives us a hope that He is with us and for us. God's love continues to paint His picture across the sky and across our hearts. His awe and wonder are found in His love. We see the overwhelming love of a God who is kind and has continued to seek and save that which was lost. To walk in forgiveness just as God has forgiven us is the most freeing feeling in the world. Jesus is the standard and example of how we are to love others. His love will endure to the end.

1 Corinthians 13:4 *"Love is patient and kind. Love is not jealous or boastful or proud."*

Personal Reflections

As Jesus has forgiven us of our sins, who is it that may
have wronged you that you need to forgive?

Write a prayer today asking for God to help you forgive
this person or people.

_____

_____

_____

_____

_____

_____

_____

_____

_____

_____

_____

_____

_____

_____

_____

_____

_____

Day 28

A Wellspring

Just about a mile up the road there is a beautiful nature trail that stretches along the water. It's a great place to go especially in the summer months, to spend some quiet time with the Lord. There is a healing that takes place in the mind by stepping away from the busyness of life and spending time in the Word of God. The freedom that comes from time in the secret place with the one who formed you gives a peace that passes all understanding. There is a supernatural renewing that takes place in the mind by the time spent in the Book of Life. Scriptures will begin to be highlighted as words of Truth that are alive and powerful. It will pierce right through your very heart and create a wellspring of living water that is found in Christ.

John 7:38 *"Anyone who believes in me may come and drink! For the Scriptures declare, 'Rivers of living water will flow from his heart.'"*

Personal Reflections

Where has God highlighted for you to go and spend some time in the Bible?

Have you felt healing in areas of your life meditating on God's word? In what areas?

_____

_____

_____

_____

_____

_____

_____

_____

_____

_____

_____

_____

_____

_____

_____

_____

_____

Day 29

How Much More?

Where I live there are many very brave black squirrels. These courageous little guys will trot right up to your porch and almost eat right out of your hand. I remember noticing one pick up a full piece of pizza in his travels and I couldn't help but snap a picture. The Lord provides even the birds, how much more will he provide for us who are made in His image. Jesus supplies all our needs every day. I don't recall a day that I was without the food that I needed to survive. But God doesn't stop there. He is a healer of the heart and mind. He supplies a mending and a renewing where He breathes new life into us by the power of his Holy Spirit. Jesus came so that we may have life and life more abundantly. God does this so much to where all we can do is thank Him with a shout of praise for just how great he is. There is no need to worry about tomorrow for today is a present given to us by God.

Matthew 6:26 *"Look at the birds. They don't plant or harvest or store food in barns, for your heavenly Father feeds them. And aren't you far more valuable to him than they are?"*

Personal Reflections

In what ways has God continued to meet all your needs?

Write a prayer today to thank Him for all the blessings that are given. Name each one.

_____

_____

_____

_____

_____

_____

_____

_____

_____

_____

_____

_____

_____

_____

_____

_____

Day 30

Kingdom Come

There are prodigal sons and daughters who today are still lost in the wilderness. We each who have been redeemed can go out to help to seek and save that which is lost just as Jesus did. He is calling us today to go forth and share the free gift of salvation that has been freely given to us. As you go into the marketplace or to your job ask the Lord if He will highlight someone for you to speak to. There is always someone who needs prayer and as we come together in faith, we will see the Father open the floodgates of Heaven. Who is the Lord putting on your heart today to go and spread the love of Jesus? It could be a neighbor, friend, coworker or maybe someone in your own family. Today let the treasure hunt begin and you will watch how the Lord will use you to bring His Kingdom to Earth as it is in Heaven.

Proverbs 3:5-6 *"Trust in the lord with all your heart do not depend on your own understanding. Seek his will in all you do, and he will show you which path to take."*

Personal Reflections

Where is God calling you to go out to share the love of Jesus Christ?

What are some creative ideas for ministry where you can go be the hands and feet of Jesus?

_____

_____

_____

_____

_____

_____

_____

_____

_____

_____

_____

_____

_____

_____

_____

_____

It is my hope that you will find the true treasures that are found only in God. For the reader of this book a great journey awaits you for the King's mission. There is new life found in a mercy that renews each morning by God the Father. Today, if you haven't accepted Jesus into your heart, I would like to leave you with a way to do so. It will be the best decision you have ever made and will be the beginning of a treasure hunt to the kingdom of Heaven.

Lord, Jesus I admit that I am a sinner and ask for you to come into my heart and into my life. I believe that you died for my sins and that you rose from the grave. I believe in my heart and confess with my mouth that you are Lord. Thank you Lord Jesus for saving my life and my soul.

"To all who did receive him, who believed in his name, he gave the right to become children of God, who were born, not of blood nor the will of the flesh nor of the will of man, but of God." John 1:12-13

Made in the USA
Middletown, DE
31 October 2023

41656607R10043